Halloween
JACK-O'-LANTERNS

Halloween
JACK-O'-LANTERNS

Kathryn Stevens

THE CHILD'S WORLD®, INC.

Library of Congress Cataloging-in-Publication Data
Stevens, Kathryn, 1954– .
Halloween jack-o'-lanterns / by Kathryn Stevens.
p.   cm.
Summary: Describes the origin of Halloween and the
meaning behind jack-o'-lanterns and other customs
connected to this holiday, as well as discussing
the cultivation and uses of pumpkins.
ISBN 1-56766-641-8 (alk. paper)
1. Halloween—Juvenile literature.
2. Jack-o'-lanterns—Juvenile literature.
[1. Halloween. 2. Jack-o'-lanterns. 3. Pumpkin.]   I. Title.
GT4965.S74   1999
394.2646—dc21   98-52030
                    CIP
                    AC

Photo Credits

© AP/Wide World Photos: 29
© ARCHIVE PHOTOS: 13
© Cheryl R. Richter: 16, 26
© 1993 Dan Dempster/Dembinsky Photo Assoc. Inc.: cover
© David Falconer/Tony Stone Images: 23
© 1994 David F. Wisse/Dembinsky Photo Assoc. Inc.: 20
© David N. Davis: 24
© Ernst Haas/Tony Stone Images: 10
© Henryk T. Kaiser/TRANSPARENCIES, Inc.: 2
© Jim Corwin/Tony Stone Images: 19
© 1997 Jim Nachel/Dembinsky Photo Assoc. Inc.: 6
© 1997 Larime Photo/Dembinsky Photo Assoc. Inc.: 30
© Michael Moore/TRANSPARENCIES, Inc.: 9
© Ron Sherman: 15

On the cover...

Front cover: This glowing jack-o'-lantern reminds people of Halloween.
Page 2: These jack-o'-lanterns are carved with silly faces.

Table of Contents

You are walking along on a cold, windy night. Ahead you see two eyes and a mouth glowing softly in the darkness. You come closer to look at the spooky, glowing face. Yellow candlelight flickers through huge eyes and a gap-toothed grin. What is this strange sight? It's a jack-o'-lantern!

⇐ This jack-o'-lantern was carved with a spooky face.

What Are Jack-o'-Lanterns?

Long ago, strange lights moving through the dark were sometimes called jack-o'-lanterns. But today, jack-o'-lanterns are Halloween decorations made from big orange pumpkins. People carve a face into the side of a pumpkin. Then they put a candle in the pumpkin's hollow inside. The candle makes the jack-o'-lantern's face glow in the dark. On Halloween, many people decorate their porches or steps with pumpkin jack-o'-lanterns. Others use plastic jack-o'-lanterns or hang up pictures of jack-o'-lanterns.

These jack-o'-lanterns are sitting on some steps in front of a house. ⇒

There are many stories about the Halloween jack-o'-lantern's beginnings, or **origin.** The most famous is an Irish folk tale about a man named Jack. Jack was a nasty man who was also very **stingy,** which means that he hated to spend money. According to the story, the Devil tried to trick Jack into giving him his soul, but Jack tricked the Devil instead. After Jack died, Heaven wouldn't take him—and neither would the Devil! Instead, Jack was forced to wander the earth in darkness, carrying a lamp. He became known as "Jack-with-a-lantern"—the origin of "jack-o'-lantern."

How Did Halloween Get Started?

Halloween grew out of a number of very old practices, called **traditions.** Over 2,000 years ago, *Celtic* (KELL-tik) people in northern Europe held a yearly festival to honor their dead. They held this festival on November 1, the first day of the Celtic year. Later, Christians started celebrating November 1 as "All Saints' Day" or "All Hallows' Day," also in honor of the dead. October 31 was called "All Hallows' Eve"—the origin of the name "Halloween." Many people believed that the spirits of the dead came back at this time of year. They also believed that witches, ghosts, and other evil spirits roamed around, causing trouble.

This very old drawing shows a witch and her cat flying on Halloween. ⇒

By the 1800s, people were taking these festivals less seriously. Especially in America, they began treating Halloween as a fun autumn holiday. They decorated their homes and held parties to celebrate. Though they still told stories about ghosts and witches, people no longer believed that evil spirits roamed the streets on Halloween. Instead, it was children who roamed the streets—playing pranks!

These children are dressed up in costumes to go trick-or-treating. ⇒

Why Do We Have Jack-o'-Lanterns on Halloween?

In earlier days, people wanted to protect themselves from ghosts and other evil spirits on October 31. They put out food and other treats to keep the spirits from getting angry. They also tried to frighten the spirits away. They dressed in costumes and set out lanterns with carved faces to represent the dead. They made the lanterns by carving out a vegetable called a **turnip** and placing a candle inside. These carved turnips were the first Halloween jack-o'-lanterns.

⇐ This bunch of turnips was grown on a farm in Nebraska.

Why Are Jack-o'-Lanterns Made from Pumpkins?

When Irish settlers came to North America in the 1800s, they brought with them the story of Jack and his lantern. They also brought their traditional ways of celebrating Halloween. But North America had few turnips for making carved lanterns. Instead, the new settlers found something better—pumpkins! Unlike turnips, pumpkins were already hollow. That made them perfect for holding a candle. Carving a face into the side of a pumpkin made a wonderful lantern.

Smaller pumpkins like these are easy to carve. ⇒

Pumpkins belong to the same vegetable family as squashes and gourds. There are many different kinds of squashes, from bright green zucchini to dark green acorn squash to bright orange pumpkins. Gourds have a harder outside skin. Cucumbers and melons are related to pumpkins, too.

Pumpkins themselves are actually the fruits of the pumpkin plant. Inside each pumpkin are the seeds for making dozens of new plants. One early Massachusetts settler accidentally dropped and broke a pumpkin in his field. The next year, he had 266 pumpkins—all of them grown from the seeds of the pumpkin he dropped!

⇐ Many markets sell fresh squashes and gourds like these.

How Else Can Pumpkins Be Used?

Pumpkins are good for more than just making jack-o'-lanterns. They are also very good to eat! Large pumpkins make great jack-o'-lanterns, but they are often tough and dry to eat. But smaller, moister pumpkins are tasty and tender. They are also good for making a favorite Halloween and Thanksgiving treat—pumpkin pie! Pumpkin seeds are nice to eat, too. Some people who carve jack-o'-lanterns save the seeds for eating. Cleaned, roasted, and salted, the seeds make a tasty snack.

Some crust shaped like a jack-o'-lantern's face tops this pumpkin pie. ⇒

Native Americans were growing pumpkins and other squashes and gourds long before European explorers came to the New World. In fact, Native Americans grew gourds as early as 9,000 years ago! They grew edible squashes as early as 5,000 to 6,000 years ago. When European settlers arrived, they learned about pumpkins and other squashes. Soon they were growing these new crops alongside the crops they had brought from Europe.

← These fresh pumpkins are ready to be sold at a farmer's market.

Pumpkin plants and their relatives have great big leaves. They also have long, winding stems called **vines.** Pumpkin vines can easily grow to 10 feet long or even longer. They can completely take over a small garden! Some home gardeners "train" squash plants to grow up fences or frames instead of spreading all over the ground. Other gardeners grow varieties of squash that have been specially grown to form smaller, bushier plants. And some people just let their squash plants run wild!

⇐ It is easy to see the winding vine of this pumpkin.

How Big Can Pumpkins Grow?

Some people like to see just how large a pumpkin they can grow. They even hold contests to see who can grow the biggest pumpkin. So far, the biggest pumpkin ever grown weighed 1,092 pounds! Many giant pumpkins grow 20 to 30 pounds every day.

It takes lots of work to grow a pumpkin that size. You must start with good soil and special seeds. Then you must add lots of plant food (called **fertilizer**), the right amount of sunlight, and plenty of water. You must also protect the plant from pests and damage. But with hard work, good weather, and lots of luck, you might just grow the biggest pumpkin in the world! Even if your pumpkin is not very big, it can still make a wonderful home-grown jack-o'-lantern.

This 1,092-pound pumpkin is the biggest ever grown. ⇒

The next time you are out trick-or-treating, take a close look at the jack-o'-lanterns you see. Which ones do you like best? The ones with scary faces? The ones that look fierce? Or the ones that are smiling? No matter what they look like, they are all saying one thing— "Have a Happy Halloween!"

Glossary

fertilizer (FER–tih–lye–zer)
Fertilizer is the food a plant uses to grow. Giant pumpkin plants need a lot of fertilizer!

origin (OR–ih–gin)
The beginning of something is called its origin. The origin of the Halloween jack-o'-lantern lies in an old Irish folk tale about a man named Jack.

stingy (STIN–gee)
Stingy people hate to spend their money or give it away. Jack-o'-lanterns are named after a folk-story character who was stingy and mean.

traditions (truh–DIH–shunz)
A tradition is a way of doing things as people have done them for a long time. Our Halloween celebrations include many old traditions.

turnip (TUR–nip)
A turnip is a kind of vegetable with a round, whitish root that you can eat. Long ago, Irish people made lanterns by carving out turnips and putting a light inside.

vines (VYNZ)
Vines are long, weak-stemmed plants that climb up things or creep along the ground. Pumpkins grow on large vines.

Index